THE CLARITY FACTOR

THE CLARITY FACTOR

FOUR SECRETS OF TRUE UNDERSTANDING

Ray DiZazzo

Granite-Collen

Published by Granite-Collen Communications
P.O. Box 621, Camarillo, CA 93011

Library of Congress Cataloging-in-publication Data
DiZazzo, Raymond
The Clarity Factor: Four Secrets of True Understanding
Raymond DiZazzo

    p.   cm.

ISBN: 0692772669
ISBN 9780692772669

     1.   Personal Communication 2. Business Communication.
           2. Communication in Management
     I.   Title.

HF57.8 .D597   2000
658.4'5—dc21
00-024736
Printed in the United States of America
BG   10   9   8   7   6   5   4   3   2   1

To Patti.

CONTENTS

INTRODUCTION

REGARDLESS OF WHAT each of us does for a living, we are all in the communication business. How clearly we speak and listen directly affects not only the opportunities that come our way, but also the level of personal satisfaction and happiness we achieve as human beings.

In a study which polled top executives in fifty-eight of America's largest companies, every single executive named communication skills as a major factor in their advancement. Graduates of business schools continually report that communication skills are the most valued training they've received. And studies on divorce and human interactions prove time and again that poor communication is a major factor in failed relationships.

Though most of us are aware of these types of studies, we rarely place the importance on communication skills they deserve. Instead, we go through life wrestling with dozens of other *seemingly* unrelated issues -- finances, personal relationships, child rearing conflicts, work relationships, career decisions and so on. As we struggle through the weeks and months grappling with these day to day concerns, we never stop to consider that how well we verbally express our own ideas and understand the ideas others express to us affects our lives profoundly.

The Clarity Factor is an attempt to refocus our attention. My aim in writing this book is to create an awareness of how proper use of verbal communication skills can not only calm and streamline your day to day life, but also expand your sensitivity to the subtle dynamics that govern all human interactions.

The four key "Focal Points" on which *The Clarity Factor* is based bring to light one critical, but often overlooked element in the verbal communication process – what I refer to as the Clarity Factor.

You might think of the Clarity Factor as the key ingredient in a complex recipe. As a whole, the recipe is verbal communication – a rich, varied and at times even exotic blend of words, gestures, emotions, body language, opinions, preferences and many other influences that guide us through the continual stream of human interactions we take part in.

The key ingredient in this recipe is a subtle, but essential element that makes verbal communication so productive and rewarding when it's at its best -- brilliant clarity of word and thought.

When the recipe is a perfect mix, we speak and we are understood; we listen and we understand. When the mix is wrong, we certainly continue speaking and listening, but a good deal of the "flavor" of our communication is lost in the exchange.

Those who become aware of the mix, and apply its principles as a paradigm for their relationships, enjoy an extraordinary ability to get their ideas across, both on the job and in their personal lives. As you might guess, the benefits they reap are equally extraordinary. Verbal communication becomes a comfortable and rewarding process. Common frustrations are avoided. Stress is reduced. Time is saved. And interactions on the job and at home take on a new and exciting sense of human connection.

As important as day to day communication skills may be, however, my hope is that you will discover something more on these pages – an unexpected, almost spiritual bi-product of that human connection.

That bi-product is an amazing, crystal clear view into a state that too often flashes by us as a momentary spark in the blur of our competitive, fast paced lives – the state of true human understanding.

In a word, then, *The Clarity Factor* is about *people* -- you and I, what our words *really* mean, how we *really* feel when we say them, and most of all, our intense desire to be heard and understood as human beings.

CHAPTER 1

NOT A GREAT DAY

GLORIA DONOVAN KICKED off her slippers, pulled back the covers, and eased herself slowly between the sheets. As she tucked herself in, she thought back over the day. It hadn't been just bad, it had been a three-in-one *disaster*- a wife's, mother's, and accounting administrator's worst nightmare.

The trouble had begun, as it often did these days, with Martin Shelby, one of Gloria's staff accountants. He had spent the day miscalculating important figures, mistreating some of the company's most valued clients, and bombarding Gloria with his usual stream of disruptive insinuations: Wouldn't it be nice if everyone, managers *and* hourly people, got long lunches? Weren't wages and benefits twice as good at most *other* accounting firms? Shouldn't a good supervisor be *consistent* with the dress code?

Then there was Bill, her "loving" husband. Mr. Considerate himself. Somewhere, in a book on the etiquette of husbands and wives, Gloria was sure there had to be a rule that read:

A husband is allowed to forget his
wife's birthday once, but *never*, having
been made aware of the error of his ways,
is he allowed to forget that birthday twice.

That, however, is exactly what Bill had done. Never mind
that she had tactfully reminded him of her birthday a
week ago. Never mind that when he had dropped by the
office on his way to a meeting there were flowers, can-
dies, and cards all over her desk from the people at work.
And, never mind that Martin Shelby's face had beamed
with spiteful satisfaction when he saw Bill absentmindedly wander out the door without so much as a *whisper* of
the words "Happy Birthday."

A barrage of other particularly stressful client problems had added to this little package throughout the
day - missing files, account mix-ups, computer software
snags, and surprise tax audits, to name a few.

And finally, to tie the bow, came Todd, the seventeen
year old stereo king of Applegate Circle. Todd the unpredictable, who earlier that evening had decided that
any mother who wouldn't allow her son to triple pierce
his left ear was mentally inadequate. He had said exactly
that, but in much worse terms, then slammed the door,
stomped out to the curb, and sped away in a cloud of
smoke and heavy metal thunder.

"Yup," Gloria whispered to herself, "three disasters
in a row. How depressing. How typical." And with these

thoughts in mind, she turned off the light and closed her eyes.

Ten minutes later she was drifting downward into a strained, uncomfortable sleep....

CHAPTER 2

THE DREAM

GLORIA FOUND HERSELF walking into a large, dark seminar room. Dozens of shadowy figures were standing in small groups chatting as if in the midst of a break between speakers. A mature, blond man stepped up to her from between two young executive types.

"Have a seat," he said to Gloria, and took her hand, motioning to the chair behind them.

Gloria turned, sat, and suddenly found they were in conference room 1-C at Smith, McCallum & Dolve - the large corporation she worked for!

Seated with them at a conference table were two figures. The first was none other than her "favorite" employee, Martin Shelby. The other person was *her*- or rather an *image* of her! Gloria's double was staring straight across the table at the image of Martin. The two looked perfectly lifelike, but they sat quietly, as if frozen in time.

In front of the real Gloria sat a strange, high-tech looking machine with an arc-shaped keyboard and two glossy black plates the size of small TV screens. The characters on the keyboard were pulsing with a light aqua glow, and for some reason, the plates seemed to be resonating or vibrating slightly at a high rate of speed. Gloria found it difficult to focus her eyes on them.

Seated next to her, also in front of the machine, was Joel ... *Joel*! That was the stranger's name! How she suddenly knew that was a mystery to her, but she turned to him and said, "Joel, what is all this?"

He smiled. "This," he said, gesturing to the high-tech machine, "is what I call the Clarity Monitoring System."

"The what?"

"The Clarity Monitoring System - a game, I guess you could say. A kind of communication game." He pointed to a red, oval button on the keyboard labeled TRANSMIT and said, "Push that button."

Without thinking, Gloria pushed it.

She was startled to hear her own voice!

The instant the button was pushed, the image of her seated down the table turned to the image of Martin Shelby and said, "Martin, I need the Connor files, ASAP."

She waited for the image of Martin to make a wise-crack, but it didn't. Something else happened. The black plates on the machine in front of her suddenly began to hum. Then they lit up.

"Inside" of one, which was labeled SENDER, a perfectly clear holographic image appeared, hovering in the darkness. It was her, seated in her office at work. She was behind her desk organizing her calendar, looking very busy and professional. Martin was standing in front of her desk. He looked fresh and relaxed, but had that usual scrunched, sour look on his face. In his arms were three bulky folders, which she knew contained the Connor financial records. He was handing them over to her.

"Inside" the other plate, labeled RECEIVER, a similar holographic scene had appeared, but with certain distinct differences.

It also showed Martin in Gloria's office. But in this scene, she was leaning back in her chair with her feet propped up on her desk, which, by the way, was clear except for a bottle of nail polish remover and a Tom Collins decorated with a tiny pink umbrella. She was chewing gum (popping it between her teeth), slowly pushing back the cuticles on her fingernails, and casually sipping her drink. She looked arrogant, mean, and bored.

Martin, on the other hand, looked exactly the opposite. He appeared frazzled and sweaty, with his tie loose and his sleeves rolled up. He looked overworked and mistreated, but there was also a look of loyalty and dedication about him. If Gloria had been asked to sum up the image he portrayed, she would have had to say that he looked like a nice, hardworking guy at the mercy of a lazy, arrogant boss.

After a moment of total confusion, what Gloria was seeing became clear to her. The holograms were showing visual impressions of her understanding of what she had just said, and Martin's understanding. Her impression appeared in the plate marked SENDER and Martin's appeared in the one marked RECEIVER. Obviously, there was a *big* difference.

Just then an electronic bell, similar to the ones used to signal the seatbelt lights in airplanes, chimed pleasantly. As it did, a rectangular glass plate "window" below the two plates lit up. A glowing, blue series of letters and numbers floated out from it:

$$CF - 18\% \quad RQ - 20\%$$

"Clarity Factor and Receptivity Quotient," Joel said.

"What?"

"That's what the CF and RQ measure. The holograms are showing--"

"I know what they're showing!" Gloria snapped. "And just what does all this mean?"

"It means you've got some learning to do."

"What kind of learning?"

"Communication learning."

Gloria was offended. "I *know* how to communicate." she said.

Joel pointed to the hologram in the RECEIVER plate. "Couldn't prove it by old Marty, there."

"First of all," Gloria responded, "being a professional management person I would never say this in public, but between you and I -- and since you don't even really exist in the first place -- Martin Shelby is a walking turmoil machine. He finds fault with everything in existence. And second, as I just said, I am well aware of how to communicate since I've been practicing daily for thirty-eigh. . . I mean thirty-six years!"

Joel smiled. "Relax," he said. "Of course you know how to communicate. Everyone does. The question is at what level of *clarity* do you communicate? This is a way to find out exactly what your clarity factor is. And who knows, if we're lucky, maybe we can bring it a bit more into focus."

"'Clarity Factor'? 'Focus'? I've got a better idea. Why don't we forget all that and just give old Marty a boot in the duff so he can be a little productive for once."

Again Joel smiled. "Aside from the 'boot in the duff,' as you put it, that's precisely what we're going to do, make Marty more productive. That and help you out a little on the home front."

"The *what?*... And just who do you think --"

"But don't worry about that now," Joel quickly inter-rupted. "Tonight we're focusing on the Martin Shelby's of the world. We'll start with a few definitions and Focal Point One.

First off, let's—"

"Now wait just a darn minute," Gloria said. "As I just made *perfectly* clear to you, I am more than capable of communicating on my own. If I weren't, I'd never have been able to run the corporate gauntlet and gotten where I am."

"Gauntlet?" Joel said. "Now there's an interesting word choice."

"That's exactly what it was. A no-holds-barred line up of company barracudas. The people I've had to compete with. People who would have loved to see me fail... and who almost got their way a few times, I might add."

"Do I sense a bit of resentment in that statement?"

"Not at all," Gloria said. "In fact I respect their abilities. It's just the nature of the beast. We all compete, and the winners get ahead. But it's no cake-walk."

"Sounds like some pretty rough times along the way."

"*Plenty* of rough times." Gloria thought back for a moment, then continued, "Some when I thought I didn't really have it in me. But I didn't fold, I surprised them. I did exactly what they did."

"Which was?"

"I got tough."

"I see," Joel responded. He paused, then asked, "And do you think there's any chance that maybe this 'toughening up' of yours might have influenced your communication style?"

"Sure. It forced me to be direct. No nonsense, just the facts. Do it."

Joel nodded. "Exactly," he said. "Well, let me throw out a theory here. And do me a favor, be honest with yourself as you think about this."

"Shoot," Gloria said.

"Just suppose this 'no nonsense' directness you've developed as a kind of corporate survival mechanism has become a little *too* cursory. Any possibility that by being so . . . terse, you might be leaving out some of what really needs to be said to the people you work with? Marty, for instance?"

Gloria thought back. She had to admit Joel's theory had a certain validity. Most of the bosses she'd worked for and the people she'd competed with over the years hadn't been the kind to explain much. Things were always too busy. It was "Handle this", "Cover that", "Just take care of it."

She recalled vivid memories of how that had resulted in a good deal of wasted effort and grappling for direction on her part. But she'd always come through. And she had to admit that she had adopted a style much the same. "Why?" she asked herself now. The answer came immediately. In order to compete, of course. To be like them. Tough. Results oriented. An achiever. But had there been a downside? . . .

Joel read the look of recognition on Gloria's face. He smiled. "Tell you what," he said, "why don't we just play the game and see where it takes us. You've got nothing better to dream about anyway, right? And who knows? It might just turn out to be worthwhile."

Why Gloria was suddenly inclined to trust this stranger, she was not sure. But for some reason, she did trust him. And somewhere inside, she knew it was the right thing to do. What she didn't realize yet was just how profoundly or how soon this new friend would change her entire life.

CHAPTER 3

THE CLARITY FACTOR

JOEL POINTED AT the black holographic plates. "These are the clarity Image Plates. They produce 3-D scenes from words -- verbal messages transmitted from a speaker," he pointed at the SENDER plate, "to a listener," he pointed at the RECEIVER plate.

Then he pointed at the rectangular glass window below the two plates. "And down here is the Clarity Factor and the Receptivity Quotient generator - it analyses each scene and quickly calculates numeric indications of how clear the message was received and how receptive the listener is likely to be to it."

Gloria hesitated. "Looks like my no nonsense style didn't work so great," she said sheepishly.

Joel acknowledged with a glance. "In your mind, it was a typical business request. To Marty, on the other hand, it was just another example of what he considers wasted time he doesn't have. You see, in his eyes you're arrogant, callous and have nothing to do. He views himself, however, as being overworked and unappreciated, but doing the best he can."

Gloria pouted.

"You see, Gloria," Joel continued, "as I just said, like most people, you know how to communicate, but you've never been taught that there are degrees of *clarity* created communication."

"You mean how well people *understand* what I say?" Gloria asked.

"Exactly," Joel continued, "the higher the clarity factor of whatever message we send - the more *precise and visual* it is - the better people will understand us. And the same thing holds true in reverse. If we listen with clarity, we're better able to understand the messages we *receive*."

"Sounds reasonable enough," Gloria said.

"But here's the catch," Joel continued. "There's always a personal barrier - what I call a *distortion factor* – created mostly by people's opinions, values, and past experiences."

"Give me an example."

"Okay, here's a simple one. If you wanted to communicate to me that a person you know is small, you'll have a mental image of what you're about to say. A gauge of what small is to you. But I also have a 'small' gauge, so to speak. It's been formed by *my* opinions, values, and past experiences. And my definition of small may be different from yours. It may be twice as big as your definition. So when you say, 'Bob is small,' the image you want to convey is *distorted* by me. I see *my* version of small, not yours."

Gloria nodded.

"So the idea is to learn to penetrate or overcome these barriers in other people -- or in yourself if you're receiving the message. In this way, you communicate according to a set of rules that creates images with maximum visual clarity in the receiver's mind." He paused and thought for a moment. "In fact, what I just said happens to be very close to an actual definition of verbal clarity, or what I call the Clarity Factor."

"What exactly is this definition?" Gloria asked.

Joel began to type. As he did, the glowing images on the plates disappeared and the following message came up on both:

THE CLARITY FACTOR
A measure of how clearly a person
speaks and listens based on
four key Focal Points

"Even to the Martin Shelby's of the world?" Gloria asked.

"*Especially* to the Martin Shelby's of the world. And keep in mind, it's not just *terse* communication styles that often lack clarity. It's unfocused or distorted communication in general. That can be a fault in almost any style. And it's not just on the job."

It all seemed to make sense. But Joel's " . . .not just on the job" comment reminded Gloria of something bothersome. "What was that stuff you said earlier about the 'home front?'"

"Doesn't it stand to reason that clarity in your personal communication can also make for a better life *off* the job, especially with people like your teenage whirlwind 'Todd the unpredictable'?"

"Unpredictable" was the perfect description. "I guess so," she said.

"And if I'm right on this, things haven't been exactly, shall we say, 'peachy' between you and your husband Bill for a while."

She was embarrassed. "But that's something else," she said. "Life's been crazy. We've just both been too busy to really. . ."

"Communicate?"

"Okay, maybe we haven't talked a whole bunch."

"Right. Now ask yourself a question. And again, be honest. Isn't the world filled with people in exactly the same boat as you? People who communicate in half-formed bits and pieces? Overworked people who talk and interact on the run? Frustrated and sometimes even angry people who are talking and listening all the time, but who don't really understand what's happening to the verbal messages they're sending and receiving? People who want desperately to be heard and even more important to be *understood*? Or, people moving through their lives rambling constantly, but not saying much of anything meaningful at *all*?"

Gloria considered this statement. It sounded close to home.

Home! Suddenly she saw a crystal clear image from her childhood. It was early morning. Summer. Sunlight poured though the kitchen, garden window. She was a small girl sitting at the table drinking orange juice and eating her cereal. Her father sat across from her, his face buried in the newspaper. Her mother sat just to Gloria's right, quietly sipping coffee and occasionally making a comment, but. . .but nothing much was really being said. Ever! Her father's face was always hidden behind page D-1 – the Sports section. And her mother always made quiet small talk. Just like her. . .and *Bill*! . . . Had she accepted Bill's detached silence all these years because it had been the norm in her childhood?

Joel had been watching Gloria intently. Suddenly, he broke her trance. "And think about this," he continued. "Wouldn't a few doses of crystal clear communication help most of those personal relationships, including yours?"

Gloria had to admit it. He was right again. This time she responded with a timid nod.

"Okay then. Good. Tonight let's start with Marty. I'll explain exactly what happened with this little faulty communication you two just had. Then I'll teach you Focal Point One of the Clarity process."

Gloria settled in at the conference table. She knew something good was happening.

CHAPTER 4

FOCAL POINT ONE

THEY TURNED THEIR attention back to the Image Plates, Gloria on one looking composed and managerial, and on the other looking like an arrogant tyrant. She pointed at Gloria the tyrant. "Is that what he really thinks of me?"

"Right," Joel said.

"But why? I don't sit like that. And I also don't do my nails in my office. And he knows perfectly well I'd never even *consider* drinking on the job. And I don't pop my gum!"

"Because you didn't say the right thing."

"What exactly *did* I say?"

Joel reached over to the keyboard and typed in the word "Repeat". Then he touched a red button. The entire exchange repeated itself. Gloria heard herself say, "Martin, I need the Connor files, ASAP."

"And just what exactly is wrong with that?" Gloria snapped. "I told him to get me some files. I'm an accounting administrator and he's an accountant. Getting files and figures is what 'old Marty' gets paid for!"

"Right," Joel said. "So he's obligated to get you the files. How *fast* he'll get them for you is one question, and, if he has any work to do on the figures, how accurate they'll be is another."

He pointed to the Receptivity Quotient. "You see his disposition is a variable. So he'll either get them for you feeling positive about it, in which case you'll probably get them quickly and accurately, or he'll get them with a chip on his shoulder, in which case --"

"They'll show up after lunch and be half wrong."

"Marty's usual?"

"To a 'T'."

"Well, let's ask ourselves why. What is it that makes Marty act that way?"

"The fact that he's a negative person?"

"Obviously Marty has certain character traits we can't hope to change with a few words. So does every employee. But there's more to his actions than a sour personality."

"Okay," Gloria said, "then how about because he's not too well-endowed in the brains category?"

Joel grimaced. "I've got a better answer," he said. "How about because he wasn't communicated to..." he looked Gloria straight in the eye, paused, and continued, "with *clarity*." As he said this, he pointed to the Clarity Factor/Receptivity Quotient window.

"I'm not sure I buy this," Gloria said. "It puts all the blame on me."

"It's not a matter of blame," Joel continued, "nor personality nor intelligence. In a business sense, it's a matter of *benefit*."

"Benefit?"

"Right. Benefit to you. You see, although Marty's personality comes into play, if you want to benefit the most from your relationship with him, you have to try to communicate with him - clearly."

"And if I don't?"

"You don't get blamed, at least not right away. But you also don't get cooperation or productivity. You just continue to put up with Marty's animosity and lack of effectiveness. That means added stress and frustration on top of what you're already putting up with. And eventually, the blame for his shortcomings does fall on you."

Gloria thought of the many times she'd been called on the carpet for mistakes in her department. She recalled the familiar churning in her stomach that accompanied conversations with angry clients and unhappy executive bosses. She also recalled how exhausted and depressed she'd always felt when they were over. "I can identify with that statement," she said.

"And keep this in mind. Though you may not be able to change an employee's personality, you can certainly *influence* it – saving yourself a ton of headaches and frustration in the process. In fact, that's one of the most critical parts of the job for anyone who acts as a mentor or supervises people."

"I guess I agree," Gloria said. "It's up to me to put my opinions aside and communicate with him clearly, if for no other reason than to be effective at my *own* job."

"Exactly."

"Okay. So how do I do it?"

"Well, there are actually four Clarity Focal Points. We'll start with the first one." As he said this, Joel reached down to the keyboard and began to type. Both plates cleared and the following text was displayed:

FOCAL POINT ONE
✓ FOCUS YOUR MESSAGE

Gloria looked unimpressed. "Boy, now there's a profound one!" she chuckled. "And I *did* focus. I asked him to get me the Connor files. That's pretty darn clear if you ask me!"

Joel appeared unperturbed. "What exactly are the Connor files?" he asked.

"The complete financial records of a man named Art Connor. We do his accounting and taxes."

"I see. And approximately how many figures are in the Art Connor account?"

Gloria thought about it. "Well, there are, I don't know ... hundreds, I guess. Probably thousands! It's a large business. But that's not the point. When I say the 'files' I'm usually after just certain figures - mostly account totals. Marty knows that."

"And do you normally need *all* of these totals when you say, 'Get me the files'?"

"Well, no, usually I don't. Most times I'm working on one specific area. Occasionally the client calls wanting to know last month's travel expenses or depreciation figures or accounts receivable or something like that."

"So, if the case we just saw was typical, we can probably assume that 'get me the files' was the first thought that came to your mind; although, it was only one or two figures you really needed."

"Right," she said. "So what? Either way he had to get off his duff and do a little work for once."

Joel frowned. It was obvious he wasn't making much headway. Then he smiled and said, "Just for the heck of it, let's alter that statement of yours and give the new version a try on Marty. We'll see if we can make it reflect more clearly what you want."

"We can do that?" Gloria asked.

"Sure," Joel said. "That's what this game is all about. Now the trick is to do two things: *Analyze* what you want to say, and be *objective* about how you say it."

"Sounds like academic mumbo-jumbo to me," Gloria said cynically. "How's it supposed to help?"

"By analyzing what you're about to say - basically just thinking over what you really want to convey - you're able to form a clear image of your message in your *own* mind before you try sending it to someone else. You focus it."

Gloria understood. And she suddenly realized that she tended to understand very clearly just about everything

Joel said. "I think I get it," she responded. "If I'm not clear on what I say, there's no way my message can reach someone else clearly." Then a second thought popped into her mind. "It's sort of like taking a picture that's out of focus, right? If the negative is bad to begin with, there's no way to make it sharp when it's developed. It's too late at that point."

"Exactly. So the very first key in the Clarity Factor is to bring the message into focus in your own mind."

"I like that. It makes sense."

"And being *objective* cuts down on another factor that tends to weaken verbal messages - emotional content. You see, if you're emotionally biased about something, for instance how you feel personally about Marty, the message you form in your mind may be in perfect focus, but it'll be *distorted*."

Gloria was catching on quickly. "In which case, it might be perfectly clear and sharp, but it would be inaccurate," she said. She thought for a second, then continued. "A perfectly sharp image on the negative, but photographed through something like . . .a *fish-eye lens*!"

"Right again. Distorted at the source by your personal opinions, values, and past experiences. And very well said, by the way."

"I think I'm 'focusing in'," Gloria mused.

"You are." Joel continued. "Now think about Marty. Does your opinion of him affect how you *view* him as a person? And if so, does that influence how you communicate with him?"

Gloria didn't like having to admit it, but she realized her opinion of Marty did create an unpleasant image of him in her mind. And that, in turn, may have affected how she spoke to him. Because she viewed him as rude, quarrelsome and lazy, had she been even more terse with him than her other employees? As she thought about it more, she concluded that if she had been, it was probably a means of avoiding conversation with him. Conversation she feared would result in comments from him she wouldn't like. Though this discovery was troubling to her, the sudden understanding of what had really been going on between her and Marty was exciting. "Of course," she said. It *has* affected how we communicate!"

Then, suddenly, she looked troubled. "But I've got a problem – a big one."

"What's that?" Joel asked.

"Being objective I guess I can live with. It's a mindset. A way of perceiving people and how I communicate with them. And I can change that fairly easily. But this analysis business isn't practical."

"How so?"

"I'm a busy person. I've got a dozen fires going ten hours a day. Half of them are out of control, and the other half are close behind. If I'm supposed to sit down and carefully analyze everything I say, I'll get burnt to a crisp before I get a word out!"

"Good point," Joel said. "You're right. Very few managers have the luxury of carefully planning every comment they make. But with a little practice, we can all make a quick analysis of our words a habit – a mind-set just like objectivity. Or what some people refer to as a paradigm."

"A paradigm shift!" Gloria said.

"Right. And think about this. The more of a shift we make, the less we have to think on the spot while we're fighting those fires."

"Why?"

"Because things go smoother. More of the fires are under control, and lots of them can be avoided in the first place. And there are quite a few times when preparation before we speak is not only feasible, but plain old good management – staff meetings, employee meetings, customer appointments, comments about productivity, presentations, and so on. The point is, if you practice focusing your message just like you practice any other management skill, it becomes a part of your style and you reap the benefits."

Again, Joel made sense. And again, Gloria had to admit it. "Okay," she said, "I guess I can live with that."

"Good," Joel said. "Now back to that faulty message of yours." He reached over to the machine and pushed a button labeled RECALL. Gloria's original message appeared on both plates:

Message - First Attempt
Martin, I need the Connor
files, ASAP.

"Now, how shall we change your original message?" Joel asked.

Gloria looked at the words. "Okay," she said, "why not? Let's see. Make the request for only one figure, the bottom line equipment depreciation total. That's a common one."

"Definitely more accurate," Joel said.

"And while we're at it, I guess we should include the word 'please'. That's probably adding a touch of objectivity, since Marty isn't my favorite person."

"Fine," Joel said. "You're asking for only what you need and disregarding any feelings you may have about Marty as a person. That's good. How about this?" He began to type and when he was done, he pushed a button labeled REVISE. The text on the plate changed to:

Message - Second Attempt
Martin, I need one figure -
the bottom-line equipment
depreciation total from the
Connor account. Could you
please get it for me as soon as
you have a few seconds?

"Okay?" Joel asked.

Gloria looked it over. It *was* more focused and objective. "Fine," she said.

Joel pushed the TRANSMIT button.

The two Image Plates went blank and the figures seated at the conference table came to life again. Just as before, the figure of Gloria spoke. But this time it said, "Martin, I need one figure - the bottom-line equipment depreciation total from the Connor account. Could you get it for me as soon as you have a few seconds, please?"

The Image Plates hummed. Two new holograms formed. This time the SENDER image, Gloria's view of the interaction, was almost the same. She was seated at her desk receiving the information from Martin in what she considered a business-like way. However, Martin was handing her a single piece of note paper instead of several bulky files.

The image in the RECEIVER plate, Martin's interpretation of the message, was much different from the last time.

He and Gloria were in her office. Although she still had an arrogant look on her face, she was seated normally, with her feet down behind her desk. She wasn't doing her nails or chewing gum and the Tom Collins was gone. Although Martin still looked a bit frazzled, he didn't appear nearly as martyred as in the last image. In this image, just as in Gloria's, he was handing over a single piece of note paper.

Just then, the electronic bell went off again and a new set of numbers floated out from CF/RQ window:

CF - 87%   RQ - 66%

"Well," Joel said, "better."

Pointing to the RECEIVER plate, he continued. "Marty still resents you, but not as much. This time he didn't view you as quite so arrogant. He still feels your request is extra work piled onto what he's already doing, but at least he realized it's not that big of a deal - just one figure. Oh, and by the way, I think he's pleasantly surprised that you said 'please.'"

Then Joel pointed to the CF/RQ window. "And as for clarity and receptivity," he said, "both factors are improved. Not great, but not bad for one minor change. Not bad at all."

"I'll be darned," Gloria whispered to herself. "It worked!"

"Sure it worked. You applied the first Focal Point. You focused your message. You analyzed or thought about how to say it, and you said it objectively. As a result, you said the right thing and your message had a higher Clarity Factor. In this case, that clarity conveyed to Martin that it wasn't really a big job to get you one figure. It also left less room for him to imagine the worst about you personally."

"Hey, this is great!"

"Well, not too great," Joel cautioned. "The message still leaves a lot of room for improvement. An 87/66 in the CF/RQ window isn't the clearest message I've ever monitored with this thing. On the other hand, we've only applied the first focal point. We still have three to go."

Gloria thought for a second and said, "'Focus your message'.... Okay, I'll have to remember that. Simple enough. In fact, deceptively simple."

"And that's the point," Joel said. "The real key is this. As simple and obvious as that little rule sounds, most people *just don't do it*! They usually say whatever comes to their mind without giving it a second thought. They communicate on the run and they mix emotions with poorly thought out words. The result is distorted, half-focused messages zipping around the home or office like swarms of bees. And that causes major problems because the people receiving those messages just don't 'get the pictures.' What they *do* get is frustrated and confused and lots of times angry."

Again, Gloria thought back over her own management career. She remembered countless times she'd been asked to perform with no clear picture of exactly what she was supposed to do. She recalled the frustration she'd often felt and the resentment toward whichever boss had given her the assignment. How could they have expected fast, efficient results with no clear understanding of the task at hand? How wasteful! And this thought brought her again to her own management style. How many times had *she* been that deeply resented boss? There was no question that Marty resented her. And the others?

Again, Joel read her expression. "Want to see a few examples of unfocused messages?" he said.

"I guess so," Gloria said, still a bit distracted by the disturbing revelations about her image as a manager.

Joel went to work on the keyboard. When he was through typing, he pushed the red button. The plates cleared and the following quotes were displayed, one at a time:

Unfocused Messages
(Off-the-Cuff Origins)

I need help with the Simpson budget. Would you do an analysis for me?

Why is it you're always late?

I need it soon.

There's a budget meeting this Friday. Come prepared to talk about expenses.

You need to improve your productivity.

We've got to cut our costs right away.

If you don't improve your
customer relations, we're
in trouble.

The plate cleared.

"They look fairly typical, right?" Joel said.

"I've said a few in my time," Gloria admitted.

"Sure you have. Just like every other manager careening around the business world from one fire-fight to another. If you really look at them, though, you'll realize they're all vague, off-the-cuff remarks. They're made without much thought given to what the sender was *really* trying to communicate or to the other person's feelings. In terms of clarity, they're, well, they're about as clear as ... ink in a black bowl!"

Gloria chuckled. "Sounds like you thought about that remark a little," she said.

"Absolutely. Because I use the first rule all the time. And, if you use it and do nothing else, your day to day communications will be sharper, and clearer. You'll say the right things more often, and as a result, you and the people you deal with will be much more effective. You'll be scratching the surface of the Clarity Process."

Gloria pointed to the plates. "So how would you clear these up?" she asked.

"We'll talk about that soon enough," Joel said. "That gets into the other Focal Points. But first, I want to make one last point about this first rule. Let's face it, human personalities are as varied and complex as the changing situations they move through. Obviously, there are no panaceas. But a simple technique like focusing your message can *influence* those personalities in a big way -- and make them much more pleasant and productive. See?"

"I'm convinced," Gloria said. "And you know what else I'm convinced of?"

"What?"

"That you don't have quite as much control over this dream as you may think. Know how I know that?"

Joel smiled. "How?" he asked.

"Because I have to use the bathroom. And I know for a fact that no matter who you are, you are not going to be able to keep me from waking up in just a few seconds and doing that."

Joel winked. "See you soon..."

The next thing Gloria knew she was rolling out of her bed, heading for the bathroom. She had no memory of Joel, the dream, or anything that had just transpired. She felt good, though - positive or uplifted or something like that - something she couldn't quite put her finger on.

CHAPTER 5

MARTY ON THE JOB

SHE WOKE AT six. She felt great, but had no recollection of the dream. She showered, dressed, got made up, and headed to the kitchen for breakfast.

For some reason it didn't bother her much that Bill was his usual early morning self and paid almost no attention to her. She gobbled down a slice of toast and a bite of cantaloupe and planted a quick kiss on his cheek on her way out the door. Oddly enough, even the new oil stain in the driveway from Todd's car didn't disturb her. She breezed right by it, hopped into her own car, and sped off for work.

As she sat on the Ventura Freeway, inching along in rush hour traffic, an assortment of random thoughts passed through her mind: the gas bill was late. Would summer ever arrive? Roast for dinner. Tonto's rabies shot. And so on. Then, suddenly, she thought about Martin Shelby. Why, she wondered, was he such a cynic and a trouble-maker? "What's he got against the world?" she actually said out loud.

It was then that a disturbing possibility occurred to her. What if *she* was Martin's problem? What if she was doing something to tick him off? No, she decided. No way. She had always gone out of her way to be fair and consistent with him. Not that he had ever returned the favor. But, come to think of it, he had never returned much of anything, including thank you's, hello's, or a day's work for a day's pay!

She tried to put the image of Marty out of her mind, but it persisted. When was the last time she had said thank you to him, she wondered. Why, it was only yesterday, she remembered, after she had asked him to re-do the depreciation on the Alyson Corporation. And in return she had gotten his typical, red-faced, resentful grunt when he dropped the file folders on her desk.

Did he resent working for a woman? Or had she really said something to offend him? Maybe that was it. Maybe she *had* offended him. She racked her brain for several more minutes, but couldn't remember anything she had said which might have angered or offended him. She certainly hadn't babied him, but she was consistent about that with all her employees. Staying in business meant getting things done, taking responsibility and running with it. That had always been her philosophy and it had certainly proven successful so far. And although she considered him lazy and resentful, she was much too professional to have ever said anything personally derogatory to him. But had her feelings about him become obvious by the way she spoke to him?

Finally, she decided that she would at least try to be more specific and tactful in her conversations with him.

After all, he had worked for her for several years now and she knew he had aspirations of becoming a manager one day. She seriously doubted that would ever happen, but as his boss, she did owe him the courtesy of respecting him as an individual.

And with the seed of that thought planted comfortably in the back of her mind, she was pleased to see that traffic was beginning to break up. She went back to worrying about rabies shots and gas bills, and made it the rest of the way to work clipping along at a brisk 45 miles per hour.

Later that morning, Gloria's phone rang. It was Art Connor. The moment she heard his voice, a sudden wave of déjà vu swept over her. It intensified when Art asked for his bottom line equipment depreciation total. He was considering investing in some new equipment, he said, and he needed it right away.

When she called Marty into her office, the déjà vu persisted. And as she was about to say, "Martin, I need the Connor files, ASAP," the thought process on the freeway that morning resurfaced. It raced through her mind to a split-second assessment of the situation and a decision that went something like this: "Martin will surely get huffy when I ask him to pull the Connor files. He gets huffy when I ask him to do anything. He probably feels overworked and underpaid. And he probably thinks I sit in here all day spitting out orders with nothing to do myself. Actually, I really don't need all the figures, just one. Maybe I should clarify that. And I should probably say 'please,' while I'm at it."

As a result, she said, "Martin, I need one figure - the bottom-line equipment depreciation total from the Connor account. Could you get it for me as soon as you have a few seconds, please?"

To her amazement, he seemed to take the request fairly well. "No problem," he said, and headed out of the office toward the file cabinets down the hall.

Gloria thought to herself, "Maybe that was it. Maybe, if I'm a little more considerate and concise about what I ask for, he'll be more productive and we'll get along better." After Marty returned with the figure and she finished her conversation with Art Connor, she hung up the phone and picked up her pen. She leafed forward to the "Notes" section of her daily planner and found a blank page. She thought for a minute and then wrote:

Think about what you want to say
- PLAN BEFORE YOU SPEAK
- BE COURTEOUS AND OBJECTIVE.

Pretty obvious, she thought. She knew there was something good about it, though - something accurate and positive. She looked it over, whispered it to herself, and smiled. The déjà vu surfaced again briefly, and then it was gone for good.

For the next week, that obvious little statement kept occurring to Gloria, and she kept putting it into practice whenever she could. Rather than just speaking impulsively, she would take a moment to think. Usually, she found there was a way to express herself more precisely and objectively. It only took a few seconds, and it seemed to improve things. It didn't work miracles, by any means, but people –- in particular Martin Shelby -- seemed to be just a *little* more receptive to her. A little easier and more efficient to deal with.

Things were going well. In fact, her only real problem that week was Todd. He had gotten in big trouble at school for insulting a teacher. Since this wasn't a first for him, he'd nearly gotten suspended - which *would* have been a first.

By the time the week was over, she had looked at the notation in the back of her planner several times. She had even revised it several times. What she'd been doing, she decided, was actually creating messages - verbal messages. She was the sender of those messages, and the people she talked to were the receivers. With that in mind, she'd revised the statement to read simply:

FOCUS YOUR MESSAGE
- ANALYSIS
- OBJECTIVITY

"Yes," she decided on that Friday night as she slipped into bed, kissed her snoring husband, and turned off the light, "it may sound simple and deceptively obvious, but it works!"

CHAPTER 6

FOCAL POINT TWO

GLORIA WAS SITTING in a hot tub holding a drink. The water was nearly scalding and the bubbles were searing her skin. She stood up wincing, turned, and found that she was in her kitchen, stepping from the refrigerator toward the breakfast table. The drink had turned into a plate of toast. She placed it on the table next to Joel and sat down beside him.

In front of them was the Clarity Monitoring System. Beside them at the breakfast table were images of herself and Bill. Both were silent and motionless and dressed as if about to leave for work.

On the table in front of Gloria was a bowl of cereal and a glass of orange juice. One of her hands was wrapped around the juice glass and the other was on the spoon.

In front of Bill was half a grapefruit and a cup of coffee, his usual breakfast. Also in front of him was his daily planner. It appeared that he had just finished a sip of coffee, looked down at his list of 'To Do's' for the day, and been frozen in that instant.

Gloria turned to Joel. "He's quite a husband," she said. "Successful executive, skilled socializer, provides well for his family, and just look how interested he is in his better half."

Joel chuckled. "Push the button," he said.

Gloria reached forward to the monitoring system and pushed the TRANSMIT button. The image of her looked up at the image of Bill. It said, "Todd got in trouble at school again, Bill. We should discuss it."

The image of Bill mumbled absentmindedly, but did not look up. The clarity Image Plates hummed and came to life.

In the plate marked SENDER, a tired and dejected-looking image of Gloria stood beside her husband in his downtown office. She had placed one hand on a stack of his files. With the other she held her temple as if a major tension headache was setting in. She appeared to have been pleading with him about something for some time. Obviously, she was having no luck getting his attention.

He, however, appeared to have no intention of acknowledging her. Instead, his attention was focused entirely on huge stacks of marketing folders, which he shuffled through while punching endlessly away at a desktop calculator. He looked cold, arrogant, and heartless.

The RECEIVER plate contained no image on it at all, at least that's what Gloria thought when she first looked at it. Instead, it appeared to be glowing inside with electronic "snow" or interference. Then, as she was about to look away, she saw something familiar surface partially through the electronic shimmering - a ghostly hologram. She continued to watch and it appeared again. There was an image after all, but only partially visible every few seconds.

It was an image of her. She was dressed in her typical business attire, but somehow she didn't look particularly business-like. She had an odd, almost dense look on her face. Her mouth looked larger than usual and she was speaking nonstop. The words were tumbling out of her mouth in rapid fire, but they were indistinguishable.

The CF/RQ window showed an equally odd 'picture'. It read:

CF - 88%   RQ - 2%

The 2% figure flickered off and on to 0%.

"What's going on?" Gloria asked Joel.

"Can't you see?" he replied.

"I can see me looking like I'm in desperate need of some spousal interaction in the SENDER plate. Which, by the way, happens to be a very accurate assessment of the situation. And I can see that the clarity factor of my statement is a pretty decent 88 percent. But the other plate is shorted out or something."

"Not the *other* one ... the *RECEIVER* plate," Joel coaxed.

"Right," Gloria said, "the RE--" And suddenly it hit her. Her message hadn't been received. She hadn't gotten through! Not only had he not given her the courtesy of agreeing or disagreeing with her, he was so wrapped up in his 'To Do's,' that he hadn't even *heard* her. It was as if she wasn't even there! Suddenly, that familiar memory of her as a young girl at the breakfast table flashed in her mind. Her father, a man she'd loved as much as she now loved Bill, sitting with his face hidden behind section D-1. Sports. And now, Bill himself. Small talk. Silence. . . It was like some horrible cycle. A vicious repetition of her childhood. She became furious. "Why, that--"

"Ah, ah," Joel interrupted. "We're here to play the game, remember? Not to say things we don't really mean."

"Game, shmame," Gloria snapped. "That inconsiderate jerk is just like my father. He doesn't even know I *exist*!"

"Of course he does," Joel rebutted. "Just like your father did. He's just too busy with other issues to give you much of his attention. You're, shall we say, a bit low on his list of priorities at the moment."

"At the moment? Bull! I'm *always* a low priority for him."

"Well, what shall we do about that?"

"I have no idea. I've tried talking to him. As you can plainly see, it just doesn't do any good. All he can think about is numbers: productivity figures, financial indices, quarterly results . . . the *Sports* section!"

"Well, I have an idea," Joel said, displaying his ever present smile. "What if we try Focal Point Two of the Clarity Factor?"

Gloria shook her head. "Here we go again with this clarity stuff." Just after she said this, she noticed that Joel paused. He seemed a bit irritated with her.

"I'm curious," he finally said. "Has the first Focal Point worked for you?"

"Worked?" Gloria wondered. "What the—" Then, suddenly she realized something. Focal Point One had worked indeed. Not in a dream but in *real life.* On the job! It had worked so wonderfully, in fact, she'd even written it down. "Ah. . .well, actually, I guess it. . ."

Joel sensed her revelation. "So I guess common sense tells us that number two might also be beneficial. Right?"

Gloria chuckled and shook her head. "You're so logical."

The irritation left Joel's face. He smiled. Then he began to type on the monitoring system. When he was done, the plates changed to read:

FOCAL POINT TWO
Magnify The Listener's Attention

"What?" Gloria asked.

"'Magnify the listener's attention.' That's Focal Point Two."

"I see," Gloria quipped. "Another real deep one...."

"But--" Joel began.

Gloria interrupted. "The point," she said, "is this. I'm his wife! He should show some common consideration and plain old courtesy. If I'm saying something, he should stop long enough to at *least* acknowledge my presence."

"And why do you think he's not acknowledging you?"

"Obviously, because he's inconsiderate."

"Wrong. He's not acknowledging you because he's unconsciously put up a communication barrier, just like we all do at times."

"Which is?"

"He's engrossed in something else."

"That's it?"

"That's plenty. In his case, it's work. In the other cases, its recollections, incoming sounds, other visual stimuli, worries, needs, concerns, the bills, the kids, the dog. Basically, any one or a combination of countless other mental barriers that don't allow incoming messages to form clear images in our minds.

"Although we may not realize it, many times we make an unconscious mental judgment that what we're doing is more important than hearing what another person is trying to say to us. We might even *try* to listen, but not really hear what's being said. In that case, we forget the words seconds later. Sometimes we even display the *appearance* that we're listening, as a courtesy of sorts to the speaker. But the truth is, in all of these cases, we're actually tuning out or rejecting the person's message because we consider it a low priority. It hasn't been conveyed in a way that--"

"Wait, I know -- that 'magnifies the listener's attention'," Gloria said with a smirk.

"Exactly! In a way that makes us, as listeners, instantly rearrange our priorities, allowing the sender's message to be number one."

"Somehow," Gloria said, "I think I'm about to be blamed for this little exchange."

"Well, let's put it this way. By using Focal Point Two, you can be the one who prevents this priority problem from happening. You can literally be assured that your message will get through."

"I see. And just how, may I ask, do I use this second Focal Point?"

"Simple," Joel said. "By making sure your message communicates at least one, better two, and sometimes all *three* of these elements." He typed on the keyboard and the plate revealed:

Interest

Importance

A request for the listener's
undivided attention

Gloria thought about it. It sounded sensible enough, but something else didn't. "I'll buy that," she said, "but what I just said to him *was* at least one of those. It was important -darned important."

"You're absolutely right. But I didn't say the message had to just *be* important. I said it had to *communicate* importance."

"Semantics," Gloria snapped.

"On the contrary," Joel said. "Does this seem to communicate importance to you?" He turned to the Clarity Monitoring System and pushed the REPEAT button. The scene replayed exactly as it had the first time. Gloria looked up and said, "Todd got in trouble at school again, Bill. We should discuss it."

Joel was right. The subject was extremely important, but the way she had said it sounded extremely *un*important. The statement came out in the same way she might have said, "Nice day out, Bill." In the same way her mother might have made small talk at the breakfast table. And just like her father, if Bill hadn't been paying attention to begin with, he would have had no idea that what she'd said was important.

"Okay, okay." she said. "Maybe it didn't sound terribly urgent."

"Right."

"So how do I fix it?"

"Why not look at our list of three elements, and you tell me." He hit another button and the following message appeared in both plates:

FOCAL POINT TWO
Magnify the Listener's Attention
✓ INTEREST
✓ IMPORTANCE
✓ A REQUEST FOR THE LISTENER'S UNDIVIDED ATTENTION

Gloria looked over the list. Interest and importance, she decided, were already part of the message. She knew Bill would be interested in what was happening to his son. It was also very important to him. He cared deeply for Todd. The only element the message didn't have was the last one - a request for undivided attention.

"Right on," Joel said, as if he'd been reading her mind. "You need to get his 'undivided attention.'" Sitting poised at the monitoring system keyboard, he continued, "Now. What shall we say?"

"I don't know," Gloria said. "I guess something like, 'give me your undivided attention?'"

"Well, you're not too far off, but that still sounds a bit, shall we say, flat. How about this." He began to type. In a moment, he pushed a button and the plate read:

Message - Second Attempt
Bill, please stop what you're
doing and listen to me. We have
to talk about something very
important.

Gloria looked it over. It definitely had more punch. "Looks good to me," she said. "Do it!"

Joel pushed the TRANSMIT button.

The image of Gloria turned again to Bill. This time it voiced the new message. And this time, several things happened differently.

First, the image of Bill immediately looked up at Gloria, instead of just mumbling.

Second, although the image in the SENDER plate was very close to what it had been the first time, the image in the RECEIVER plate was not. Now it had a clear, fully-formed image on it - an image of Gloria.

She was dressed in a business suit, just as in the last one. But in this image, she also had a business-like look on her face. Her mouth was not distorted, and she was talking at a slow to moderate pace. She appeared to be intelligent, level-headed, and obviously very concerned about something.

Gloria's jaw dropped. She had done it! She had actually gotten through to Bill. She had convinced him with one simple statement that her message was more important than what he was doing. He had rearranged his mental priorities and was now ready to communicate with her on her level. She looked down at the CF/RQ window and saw:

CF - 89%   RQ - 92%

"So do we get to talk now?" she asked.

Joel looked at his watch. "Sorry. It's seven a.m.," he said. "And you've got an. . .eventful. . . day ahead."

Just as Gloria was about to complain, she glanced down at Joel's watch. Green, digital numbers began floating out of the watch face, blinking and beeping... 7:00 ... beep ... 7:00 ... beep ... 7:00 ....

"Joel! What's--"

Beep ... 7:00 ... beep ... until she had completely surfaced out of the dream, rolled over, and hit the snooze button on her digital clock radio.

She had no recollection of Joel or the dream.

Seven o'clock, she thought to herself. Great. Another fun Saturday cleaning house.

Then she dropped back off to sleep for another three taps on the snooze button....

CHAPTER 7

BILL GETS THE WORD

LATER, GLORIA GOT up feeling well, except for one problem-- a nagging concern about Todd's near suspension from school. She and Bill had done nothing about it yet. They had both been too busy to get together and discuss it. As she busied herself with the usual weekend chores, this concern turned to plain old worry. She continued to worry as she went about balancing the bank statement, arranging for a visit by the plumber, changing the sheets, and finally, early in the afternoon, grocery shopping.

When she had finished these chores, she decided to do a little general straightening up. This led her through various household disasters in several rooms. Eventually it brought her to the study and a face-to-face confrontation with Bill's perpetual stack of business paperwork - the stack that never got cleaned up. Today, when they should be discussing their son's school problem, she was cleaning house and he was playing catch-up at the office - numbers, reports, indices.

What was it about their relationship that made Bill continually immerse himself in business and pay so little attention to her? Or was it their relationship at all?

Maybe it was just as Bill had often said, simply a necessary evil of an executive's job.

No, Gloria decided, that was not the case. Granted, an executive's job might mean a good deal of off-hours work, but it shouldn't mean paying almost no attention to your family. There should be a balance - a happy medium. So why wasn't there?

After nearly fifteen minutes of considering various possibilities, Gloria asked herself an interesting, if not obvious, question. What if Bill didn't pay any attention to her because he felt that what she had to say wasn't important, or at least not as important as his work? What if she and Todd were simply lower than the month's productivity figures on his list of priorities?

As Gloria thought about this, it seemed to make more and more sense. Bill wasn't a bad man. On the contrary, he was a very good man in many ways. He was simply a busy man. A man who was acting according to a set of mental priorities that told him his job was supposed to occupy the most important part of his general consciousness.

The next question was how to change that. She thought about the communication rule she had recently invented:

FOCUS YOUR MESSAGE
Analysis
Objectivity

Did she really know exactly what she wanted to say to Bill? That, she decided, could be any number of things. But a good subject for starters was Todd. He was some-one both of them should be talking (worrying) about, regardless of how busy they were.

As she realized this, a sudden feeling of confidence and determination prompted Gloria to do something strange. She stuck her feather duster in a flower pot, grabbed her car keys, walked out of the house, hopped in the car, and headed for Bill's office!

As she moved along the freeway, she thought about her communication rule. Focus your message. Think about what you want to say. She decided that she knew what she wanted to say to Bill about Todd, and she would clearly think out how to say it before she arrived. In this case, however, the real problem wasn't the subject of the commu-nication, but getting him on the same wavelength as her.

She wondered how she could do that. What they were going to talk about was very important to both of them. Importance, she thought, was . . .well *important*! It was something a person should always bring to a con-versation if they were going to interrupt someone. What else, she wondered? *Interest*! Of course! If she were to walk into Bill's office and start talking about his indices, he'd probably be ready to go on for hours. But she also knew he was interested in Todd.

And then another thought occurred to her. What if all she had to do to get Bill to listen to her was to *ask*?

What if she just walked in and let him know that what she was about to say was very important? Would that be enough to make him put down the calculator and listen?

She realized it probably would be, as long as what she had to say really *was* important enough to take priority over his weekend number crunching.

Of course, she thought! Another critical part of communicating was being sure that what you say is actually *heard* by the listener. To be sure of that, your words should be either important, interesting, or they should get the other person's undivided attention - tell them to listen up. Simple!

The remaining time on the freeway was just enough to allow Gloria to consider all of these ideas and put her first rule into use – formulate exactly what she would say to Bill when she reached his office. It was also enough time for her to make a mental note to jot down what she had been thinking over in her planner.

As Gloria stepped out of the elevator in the Schwartz/Hammil building and walked down the hall to the executive suites, a familiar wave of déjà vu swept over her. It intensified as she entered the suite, moved past the empty receptionist's desk, and opened the door to Bill's office.

There he was, glasses on the bridge of his nose, pen in hand, punching away at the calculator. When she stepped in he briefly looked up over the rim of his glasses and said, "Hi, hon. Out shopping?" in his usual distracted tone.

"Hi," Gloria said as she walked in. She stood beside his desk and took a deep breath. Then she said something that seemed incredibly familiar: "Bill, please stop what you're doing and listen to me. We have to talk about something very important."

To Gloria's amazement, Bill stopped calculating, put his pen down, and removed his glasses. He looked directly into her eyes and, as he did, Gloria saw something wonderful - mental connection. She was indeed on the same wavelength as Bill. She could also see that it wasn't his surprise at the tone of her voice that now held his attention, but a genuine interest in hearing what she was about to say. Her simple little introductory statement had made her first on his list of mental priorities. The numbers were forgotten. He was looking at his wife and he was attentive.

"What is it, honey?" he said, putting his work aside.

Drawing on her first rule of communication, Gloria responded with a clear and well thought-out message. She said, "Bill, Todd nearly got suspended from school for insulting Ms. Garnell again. I'm really concerned about him, and I think we need to put our heads together and decide what to do."

She noticed that Bill's eyes were still focused on hers. She hadn't lost him. In fact, he leaned forward and said, "That kid is really getting out of control. You're right. We need to talk."

So they did talk - clearly, simply, and on the same wavelength. And although Gloria was concerned about

Todd, another of her worries disappeared, at least for the moment - her concern about communicating with her husband.

Gloria remembered to refer to her planner later. She thought about her new communication rule, and after using it for several days, and revising it several times, she wrote it in under the first rule. This new one read:

MAGNIFY THE LISTENER'S ATTENTION
Interest
Importance
A request for the listener's
undivided attention

The next few days went well. She could tell that she was communicating better because she was reaping benefits from it. Her employees were clear about their assignments and they were more willing to comply with her requests. The combination of these two factors had led to reduced stress, increased efficiency, and what seemed like a more pleasant office environment for everyone. And Bill had been more receptive as well. They had actually had an interesting conversation about business trends that morning over breakfast.

The only problem remaining was Todd. She and Bill had decided to ground him, and he had been less than crazy about the idea. He had insisted, in his usual obstinate tone, that a seventeen year old was too old to ground and that he was being treated like a baby. These types of remarks led to several confrontations centering around Todd's immaturity, his inconsiderate behavior, and his increasingly rebellious attitude. Gloria and Bill somehow got through these bouts, still sticking to the disciplinary plan they had agreed on.

Then, a week later, things took a turn for the worse....

CHAPTER 8

A CONFRONTATION

IT BEGAN WITH a simple request for Todd to turn down his stereo.

Gloria had been trying to have a phone conversation with Bill, who had flown out of state the day before on business. She had gotten sick and tired of competing with hard rock music. "Turn down that noise!" she hollered, cupping the telephone in her hand.

The stereo stayed at the same deafening level.

She tried again. "I said, turn it down, Todd!"

Still no change. Finally she'd had enough. She said goodbye to Bill, hung up the phone, and stomped down the hall to Todd's room.

She knocked. No answer; just noise. She knocked again, louder. Still no response. Just as she was about to open the door, the music was turned off. A few seconds later Todd opened the door and the two stood face-to-face.

"Fine," Todd said with a sneer. "The music is off. Happy now?" He stepped past her, stomped into the bathroom and slammed the door.

Gloria fumed.

She walked to the bathroom door and said, "Oh, I see. Now I'm being overbearing because I'd like to have a simple telephone conversation with your dad without having to scream over the screeching from some punk rock group. Is that it?"

No answer.

"Is that it, Todd? Come on. I'd like to know!"

His sarcastic voice came booming through the door. "Can't I at least use the bathroom in this house without some sort of accusation?"

Gloria's fuse blew. "No," she hollered. "You *cannot* use the bathroom! Not until you open this door and apologize for the way you've been speaking to me! You get out here right now!"

No answer.

"I mean it, Todd!"

No answer.

"I've had it with you!"

Gloria was just about to say, "Fine, you're grounded for another two weeks," when the door flew open and Todd stepped to within an inch of her face. "You've had it?" he sneered. "*You've* had it?"

"You're darn right I have! Your father and I work--"

"Well, I've had it too! Right up to here!" He swept his hand across his eyes and stomped away. He went past his room and headed for the kitchen. Gloria followed in hot pursuit.

Todd opened the refrigerator and got out a can of Coke. He popped it open and began to drink. Gloria approached. "Now you just hold it right there," she said, "and listen to me!"

"That's the problem, Mom! All I do is *listen* to you - Todd, clean your room. Todd, quit driving too fast. Todd, you slept too late. Todd, turn your music down. Todd, you're a failure. Todd--"

"I have never called you a failure and you know darn well that I never would."

"Well, you might as well! Everything I do around here is wrong! And you and Dad won't take two seconds to listen to what I--"

"To what you have to say? To snide remarks and self-ish demands? For--"

Todd stepped up to her face again. Now he had gone beyond being a wise guy. He, too, was furious. "Okay, here it comes. Your real feelings, right? I'm snide and selfish and just plain no good, right!?"

"I never--"

"Yes, you did. You just said it!"

"No, I--"

"Yes, you did. You did, Mom! You did!"

"Todd, you'd just better--"

"You said it, Mom. And you know why? Because you mean it. Because your son is a failure, that's why!"

Gloria was beginning to tremble. She could feel the blood draining from her face. Her mouth was dry. She tried to respond, "I am ... your ... mo ... mother--"

"You think I'm a failure and you might as well admit it! I can't do anything right and you won't listen to a

word I say. All you care about is what *you* have to say.
That's all you've ever cared about Mom. *You! You! You!*

"I can't ... t ... take--"

"You can't take what, Mom, the truth?" As he said
this, Todd threw his Coke can across the kitchen into the
corner. It slammed into the wall beside the dishwasher
and began spewing foam all over the kitchen floor.

"Well, I don't care, Mom!" he continued. "I've just
had it up to my eyeballs with listening to you preach! Just
admit it; you think your son is a failure! A failure! A
failure!"

It was then that Gloria could find no more words.
She broke down in tears and ran for her room. She dove
onto her bed crying hysterically. Later, through convulsive sobs, she heard Todd's door close. His music started
up again, but this time it played quietly.

Gloria stayed where she was for several hours, sob-
bing herself into a deep depression and wishing Bill was
home. Finally, the sun set. Totally exhausted, she fell
into a shallow and disturbing sleep.

CHAPTER 9

FOCAL POINT THREE

As SHE WEPT and scrubbed Coke off the kitchen floor, Gloria heard a noise. She looked up and saw three long-haired, crazed-looking guitar players sitting on the backs of huge pigs dressed in police uniforms. The guitar players laughed, mumbled something about her lack of pitch, then turned and rode off into a jail cell. Gloria screamed, fell forward through the linoleum, and tumbled, still screaming, into the backseat of Todd's little yellow Volkswagen Bug.

Beside her was Joel. "Rough day?" he asked casually.

She gathered her wits and looked around. They were in the backseat of the Bug, with the Clarity Monitoring System between them. In the front seat was an image of Todd on the driver's side, and an image of Gloria on the passenger side. Both were motionless, looking as if they had been frozen in the act of watching a drive-in movie.

And, speaking of the movie, on the drive-in screen, a teenage rockumentary was playing - a series of shots of crazed rock bands, drunken concert crowds, backstage pot smoking, and bodyguard hysteria.

"Yes," Gloria responded, in a huff. "As a matter of fact, it *was* a rough day. And it looks like I won't get any relief tonight, either!"

"Now, now," Joel said. "He's just a kid going through a rough period in his life."

"Right. And he's hell-bent on making me pay for it."

"Now come on. Aren't you overstating things?"

"Overstating? Not quite. Today he treated me not just bad. Today he treated me like, like *dirt* -- like he had absolutely no respect for me whatsoever!"

"I'll have to admit, he was pretty rude."

"Not rude, heartless!"

"You see," Joel said, "lots of times this kind of resentment is what happens when kids and parents don't say the right things."

"Oh, no you don't!" Gloria said. "No way are you going to chalk this one up to that clarity business. I've been using what you taught me and it's been working great. I've been doing my best to communicate clearly and thoughtfully, and the people I deal with have been very receptive."

"You think Todd would agree with that?"

"The only thing Todd would agree with is that I'm a spiteful and unfair person whose sole purpose in life is to make him miserable."

"How come?"

"Because he's unreachable. Because he's a teenager. And because he's spoiled and disrespectful. That's why."

Joel thought about that. Finally he said, "A little spoiled, I guess I'd buy and maybe even disrespectful at times. But unreachable? You know I'm the wrong guy to tell that to!"

"Oh, I see where this is headed," Gloria said. "We're going to use some of your so-called, Focal Points to try to talk to him. Ha! Fat chance!"

Joel shook his head. "How soon we forget," he said.

"What?" Gloria snapped.

"Nothing," Joel responded. "Listen, can I ask you a question?"

"Why not?"

Suddenly, he was dead serious. "Should I push this button?" he said, pointing to the TRANSMIT button on the Clarity Monitoring System, "or should we end this dream right here and now?"

Gloria was stunned.

For the first time in her relationship with Joel, he appeared genuinely angry with her. In fact he was not just angry, he seemed ready to give up on her. "Well ..." she stuttered, "I ... I--"

"Because," Joel interrupted, "if I push this button, you've got to *want* to improve things. You've got to open up. And not just to Todd. To your *own* faults. The ones you inherited along the way as a struggling manager. The ones you brought to this family from thirty years ago sitting across the breakfast table from the Sports section.

The ones you've carried around all these years because you felt your husband was neglecting you."

Again Gloria stuttered. "I . . . I don't--"

"And I'll tell you right now," Joel continued, staring directly into her eyes. "You *won't* like what you see. From here on in, it's no. . . 'cakewalk', as you once said."

There was no other way. She knew it and he knew it. She had to say, "Yes, push the button," and he had to hang in there with her. They had come too far.

She got control of her emotions. She might have been learning a thing or two about communicating, but she was still as tough as the best of them. "Push it," she said.

Joel pushed the TRANSMIT button.

The image of Gloria turned to the image of Todd and said, "When are you going to quit being so negative and destructive and start listening to me?"

The clarity Image Plates immediately lit up.

Gloria looked at the SENDER plate first. Inside it was a scene of her seated on the bed in Todd's room. She looked very neat, composed, and in charge. There was also a look of genuine concern in her eyes and an expression of kindness and love on her face. She looked like the mature, authoritative woman she imagined herself to be, trying to share an important gem of wisdom with her cherished but ungrateful son.

And, speaking of her son, Todd was in the scene also. He was seated on the floor beside his stereo system. He was shaking his head, rolling his eyes, and snickering, as he turned the volume control on his stereo higher and higher. He swayed back and forth to the beat of the music, waving his long, scraggly hair. Occasionally, he looked directly into Gloria's eyes as if to say, "Go ahead. Keep trying. Keep trying to communicate with me. It won't do you a bit of good!"

It was perfectly obvious that he wasn't listening to a word Gloria was saying, and that he could care less about the wealth of knowledge she was trying so desperately to share with him.

She turned to the RECEIVER plate.

The shock almost floored her.

She was present in this plate also, but she looked only vaguely like her real self. She looked more like a huge, female guard in a Russian prison. She was overweight, pallid, plain, and downright mean-looking. As in the SENDER plate, she was in Todd's room, but in this version she stood tall and bulky above his bed, looking down on him.

And he was a sad-looking human being indeed. Although he looked neat, handsome, and in a way even dashing, he also looked thin, tired, and defeated. Anyone who didn't know him would have taken him to be a romantic stranger who had stumbled into some horrible trap sprung by the towering hulk of a woman standing above him.

The Moscow Moll! This was who she was to her son! She began to cry hysterically.

"Now, now," Joel said. "It's not all that bad. Remember, he's just a kid and he's got..." He glanced at the RECEIVER plate. "well, quite an imagination."

"He hates me!" Gloria sobbed. "He thinks I'm a two hundred pound prison guard for the KGB!"

Joel started to chuckle, but caught himself. "He does not hate you. He hates the way you *talk* to him. And that taints his image of you as a person."

"But what I said was true! He is negative and destructive and he won't listen to a word I say!"

"True or not," Joel said, "remember that people *distort* what we say. They put up barriers based on their own opinions, values, and personal experiences."

This made Gloria feel a little better. Not much, but at this point every little bit helped. At least it probably wasn't as bad as it appeared to be, and for once Joel had placed the blame on someone other than her. It appeared, for a moment, that this communication problem was to be Todd's.

The moment, however, was short lived.

"You'll also recall," Joel continued, "that it's up to each of *us* if we want to communicate with true clarity, to get through these barriers as much as possible which, incidentally, happens to summarize Focal Point Three."

"Okay," Gloria said, drying her eyes, "I know it's inevitable. Go ahead and tell me about Focal Point Three."

Joel typed on the Clarity Monitoring System. Then he pushed a button. The plates cleared and the following text was displayed:

FOCAL POINT THREE
✓ PENETRATE PERSONAL BARRIERS

"Believe me," Gloria said, "my son is by definition the most impenetrable barrier on the face of this planet. He could turn a Happy Birthday toast into a death wish in no time flat."

"Even if he's communicated to you with clarity?"

"Try it," Gloria challenged. "I dare you."

"There's only one thing I've ever come across that could make Focal Point Three ineffective."

"And what's that?"

"The lack of Focal Point Four."

"Which is?"

The question seemed to make Joel uncomfortable. His eyes shifted quickly away from Gloria's. "Never mind," he said. "That's a bridge you'll have to cross soon enough." He regained his composure. "Right now, let's just give number Three a shot."

"Fine," Gloria said. "Fire away."

Joel turned to the monitoring system and hit a series of buttons. The following message came up:

Message - First Attempt
*When are you going to
quit being so negative
and destructive and start
listening to me?*

"Okay," he said, "what shall we do to it?"

Gloria stared. She had no idea.

Finally Joel spoke. "I've got a great idea," he said. "This may be a tough one. And since you said the other focal points have been working for you, why don't we just apply everything you've learned up to now?"

"Fine," Gloria said. "We have to think over what it is we're trying to say to him. We have to be analytical and objective. And we have to focus our message."

"Exactly. And you're the only one who can provide those things, since you're doing the sending."

"Sounds fair enough."

"Good. What exactly do you want to communicate to your son?"

Gloria sat deep in thought for several minutes. As she pondered this question, the teenage rockumentary played violently on the screen. A swooning fan was being dragged off the stage by a motorcycle "Hell's Angels" type. A guitar player slammed his polished red instrument into a post, shattering it with an ear-splitting "SPROOOONG!" The crowd loved it.

After several moments, Joel sensed that a lightbulb had just clicked on in Gloria's head.

He was right.

She took a deep breath and spoke.

"Okay," she said. "What I really want to communicate to Todd is that I *can't* seem to communicate with him! No matter what I say or do, I just can't seem to get through!"

"Excellent," Joel said, smiling broadly. "I'd say you're right on the money, so far. But could I suggest maybe just adding one other thought to that?"

"What's that?"

"The fact that you *want very much* to communicate with him."

Gloria considered his statement. "Yes," she said. "Absolutely! I can't seem to communicate with him and I do want to very badly. That says it all."

"That's a bit different from what's on the plate," Joel said carefully.

Gloria looked at the first message. He was right. Her first words had been angry, negative, and impulsive. They had been a far cry from what she had really wanted to say.

"So that takes care of Focal Point One," Joel said. "You now have a precisely focused image in your own mind of the message you want to send, and you've done it in a way that overlooks your negative image Todd. How about number Two?"

Gloria thought and said, "'Magnify the listener's attention.'"

"Right," Joel continued. "You've got to become first on his mental list of priorities. And, if you'll recall, we said that doing that meant including at least one, and sometimes all three, of certain elements in your message."

"Interest, importance, and/or a request for the receiver's undivided attention."

"Perfect."

"Somehow," Gloria said, "I don't think Todd is particularly interested in what I have to say at this point. And I know he does he doesn't think it's important. So I guess we'd better go for the request for undivided attention."

"Right again," Joel said. "So where does that leave us?"

"At Focal Point Three," Gloria said.

CHAPTER 10

AN OPPOSITE REACTION

"IF YOU RECALL," Joel said, "I told you how people distort the messages we send."

Gloria remembered. "You used an example of an interpretation of the word 'small,'" she said. "What was small for one person might not be the same for another."

"Exactly. And I told you that people apply these distortions based on what they've come to know and trust in their own lives."

"Personal barriers?"

"Right again. So the trick in communicating a message with maximum clarity, meaning as close to the way you imagine it as possible, is to make the receiver interpret your message more by *your* opinions, values, and experiences, rather than his or hers."

"Sounds like quite a trick."

"Actually," Joel said, "one hundred percent clarity is impossible. A receiver will always include some of his or her own personality in interpreting what you say. The amount of that inclusion, however, can be greatly influenced by the speaker."

"Okay. So how?"

"There are four basic keys involved in limiting a receiver's distortion," Joel said. He typed on the keyboard and the following words came up:

Visual Language
Use of Analogies
Request for Feedback
Revision as Needed

"Okay," Gloria said, shaking her head. "Back to that big problem, again. Do these 'keys' *all* have to be a part of every message? Because if they do, I'll have to put the world on hold every time I want to say something."

"No, they don't, but usually the more the better."

"Give me an example," Gloria said.

"Okay, we'll keep it simple. Let's go back to our interpretation of the word 'small.' If I say to you, 'I have a friend who's small,' I'm not being very specific, right?"

"I guess the word 'small' by itself is a pretty general term," Gloria conceded.

"Exactly. As a result, you imagine 'small' to mean whatever it has always meant to you, right?"

"Right."

"So your personal barrier stays intact."

"Solid as a rock."

"On the other hand, if I say, 'I have a friend who has to stand on his toes to see what's on the kitchen table,' I've suddenly gotten much more visual."

Gloria 'saw' the image Joel had created in her mind. She nodded.

"You begin to 'see' the image I'm trying to send -- according to *my* parameters, rather than your own. Right?"

Gloria thought about it. "You're absolutely right," she said, still imagining the tiny person reaching onto a kitchen table.

"Barrier penetrated," Joel said with a smile. "Here are a few other examples." He typed on the Clarity Monitoring System and the following came up on the plates:

VISUAL LANGUAGE - EXAMPLE ONE

<u>VAGUE</u>	<u>VISUAL</u>
The job is super.	The job has great hours, high wages, and lots of personal reward.
She's getting really old.	She's 89, weighs only 92 pounds, and she sits hunched over in a wheel-chair.
My new car is beautiful.	My new car is a midnight blue Toyota pick-up, with chrome wheels and gray leather upholstery.

Gloria looked over the list. As usual, Joel was right. The messages labeled Visual were just that -- clear and precise.

"Get the idea?" Joel said.

"Absolutely," Gloria responded. "It's perfectly 'clear.' But I have to come back to the same problem - practicality. I don't have time to sit around all day thinking up super-descriptive ways of saying things."

"And neither do other managers and parents or husbands and wives," Joel said. "But if we make it a habit to focus on what we say, and if we realize how much more clearly our ideas are understood by others, doesn't it make sense to constantly work on improving the visual quality of our language?"

Gloria thought about this. She certainly wasn't going to enroll in a picturesque speech class tomorrow, but considering how important the clarity of her ideas could be -- the impact it could have on her job and her life -- she *could* find the time to strive for improvement.

"So just make it a point to work on it?" she asked.

"Exactly."

"Okay, that much I can manage. Now, how about the next one – the use of analogies?"

"An analogy," Joel said, "is simply a statement of similarity between two ideas. This gives the listener a point of reference from which to visualize what you're saying. For example, if I were to use an analogy to describe this small friend of mine, I might say, "I have a friend who's so small he looks like one of the Munchkins from *The Wizard of Oz*."

Gloria nodded.

"Obviously, this uses an image most of us are familiar with, a little person from a famous movie, to provide a reference for the listener. So, again, it's more precise and visual. The person tends to 'see' what you're saying according to *your* parameters rather than his. And the result?"

"Barrier penetrated."

Joel smiled, leaned over and typed on the monitoring system. "Here are a few more examples," he said. The plates lit up with:

ANALOGIES - EXAMPLE ONE

VAGUE	ANALOGY
He was a tall guy.	He was tall enough to be Magic Johnson's body double.
She's really mad.	She's as mad as a tom cat tangled in a ball of yarn.
He's very smart.	He's like a 27-year-old Albert Einstein.

Gloria checked out the list. "Fine," she said, "I get the idea. But what if I, or the person I'm talking to, has no idea who Einstein was?"

"Then that analogy is no good. That's one of the dangers in using analogies. You have to be pretty confident that your analogy means the same thing to the listener that it does to you. If it doesn't, your message either goes out of focus, or the listener's personal barrier distorts it to fit his or her mental preference. Which, by the way, brings us to the third element, 'requesting feedback.'"

"I think I can figure this one out," Gloria interjected. "If we say something that *doesn't* seem to be getting through, we can ask for feedback to see if we're being clear. Right?"

"Right. You ask a question like, 'See what I mean?' or 'Am I being clear?' or 'Get it?' If the receiver says 'no' or gives you a quizzical look or some other signal that says you're not getting through, you go directly to the last element, 'revision as needed.'"

"You change what you're saying to make sure it *is* clear."

"Exactly," Joel said. "So what do you think?"

"I think that in theory this all sounds very logical and workable," Gloria said, "from a *business* standpoint, that is. I mean, there's no way I'm going to change overnight into a communication whiz like you, but I *can* see how awareness of these keys and some practice can develop the kinds of habits that will make what I say much more clear to the people I speak with. And that's important. Actually, I'm starting to realize that it's a lot more important than I've ever imagined. If you stop and think about it, the only way I have of getting my ideas across to other people is with my words. If they're getting distorted or thrown out of focus in the transition, people are hearing things I'm *not* saying!"

"Not a very comforting thought, is it?" Joel commented. "It's scary! I mean, who knows what people have been thinking all these years as I've gone around barking out distorted, unfocused bits and pieces of what I really wanted to say."

"Nicely put," Joel said. "But you said only in a business sense?"

"I guess I meant in an *adult* sense. Most of us adults reason on a more or less level playing field. At least we have maturity and experience on our sides. Teenagers like Todd," she pointed to the image of her son in the front seat, "are on some playing field from the planet Mars. Just look at his preference in entertainment."

Joel looked up at the screen. In the rockumentary, a writhing, half-clothed drummer was kneeling on the stage as if in the midst of a convulsive seizure. He had just lit his drums on fire and was now worshipping them. The crowd was going crazy.

"The problem," Joel said, "is that Todd's playing field *isn't* level. Not yet. It's changing as he grows. And he's out there alone trying to keep his balance on it."

The word "alone" set off a kind of distant alarm in Gloria's mind. As she started to ponder it, Joel got a bit uncomfortable again. He started to say something, then thought better of it. Instead he brought the conversation back to where they had left off, saying, "Shall we see just how level his playing field is?"

"Why not?" Gloria said, still a bit distracted.

"Okay. We said we wanted to tell him that you felt you couldn't communicate with him, but you wanted to very badly."

"Right."

"And we had decided to preface that up front with a request for his undivided attention."

"Right again."

"Okay, first things first." He typed the following message into the clarity system:

Message - Second Attempt
Todd, you need to stop
thinking about everything
else and listen to what I
have to say. It's more
important than you realize.
Will you please do that for me?

"Sounds *really* important," Gloria said.

"Is it?" Joel asked.

Gloria nodded. She was beginning to realize just how important.

Joel pushed the TRANSMIT button. The image of Gloria turned to the image of Todd and said, "Todd, you need to stop thinking about everything else and listen to what I have to say. It's more important than you realize. Will you please do that for me?"

The image of Todd turned down the drive-in car speaker and looked at the image of Gloria. The plates hummed. The holograms formed.

The SENDER plate contained an image of Gloria that was similar to the last one. Somehow, though she looked more realistic and sincere. She was still seated in Todd's room on his bed. She looked calm, serious, thoughtful, and understanding. She portrayed the image of a woman who had motherhood well in hand, and who was very confident about what she was about to say to her son.

The image in the RECEIVER plate had changed drastically. The Moscow Moll was gone. In her place was Gloria, still looking a bit mean, but much more like the real her. It was obvious that changing the way she had begun her message had made a big difference in Todd's mind.

The CF/RQ window read:

CF - 95%   RQ - 73%

Gloria was extremely pleased. She was about to point out the reading to Joel, when, for just a moment, it flickered. Gloria thought she saw the 73% change to 24%. In a flash, however, 73% reappeared. She started to ask Joel what was happening. "What's--?"

"A little better, huh?" Joel said quickly.

And his smile was enough to make Gloria temporarily forget the flickering numbers. She felt like an immense and long-carried burden had been lifted off her shoulders. Todd the unpredictable was actually listening to her.

Joel continued to type enthusiastically. "Now that we're first on his list of priorities, let's see if we can capitalize on it," he said. He hit a button and the plates cleared. A new message came up. It read:

Second message - second half
Todd, lately when you and I
talk, I honestly feel like a person
lost in a foreign country
trying to talk to a stranger.
You keep nodding your head,
but I have this terrible fear
that I'm just not getting
through, no matter what I say!
That's frustrating enough by
itself, but it's even more
frustrating because I <u>want</u> to
talk to you - really talk
to you, very badly!

"What do you think?" Joel said. "Shall we send it?" Gloria looked it over. It was definitely precise. And the analogy about being in a foreign country accurately described how she felt. "Send it," she said.

He pushed the button. The image of Gloria spoke the message to the image of Todd. The image of Todd looked up. The plates came to life.

Both scenes were completely changed.

The SENDER plate showed Gloria's understanding of the message. She was standing on a dark, wet sidewalk which ran beside a cobblestone street. It looked like a cold, dreary night somewhere in Europe. She was addressing a young man who looked like Todd as several people stood nearby looking on.

She was trying to talk to the young man. What she was saying was inaudible, but the expression on her face told a story of tension, fear, and frustration. She looked lost and abandoned and it seemed she was trying to ask the young man for directions. Although he kept looking directly at her, and kept nodding slightly, he said nothing. And there was a subtle look of indifference on his face. He appeared to be letting this foolish American stranger talk herself silly, with no regard for the terror she was feeling.

When Gloria saw the picture, she felt it accurately reflected what she was trying to convey to Todd.

She turned to the RECEIVER plate and was amazed to see that it showed a similar scene.

The location was different. Instead of Europe, it looked like Mexico, with a narrow street and Spanish style housing on both sides. Gloria was there, and so was the stranger. Just as in the picture Gloria had imagined, she looked fearful and frustrated as she pleaded with the stranger for help.

In this scene, the stranger looked more like Todd, with long, dark hair. But he also had a thick, curly beard, tattoos, and wore lots of chains. He looked like a cross between her son, a rock band leader, and a romantic Mexican bandit. The look on his face was similar to the look on the face of the youth in Gloria's image. He appeared to have little interest in what Gloria was saying. In fact, he looked as if he couldn't have cared less.

The CF/RQ window chimed and formed:

CF - 87%   RQ - 48%

When both the picture and the CF/RQ reading finally sank in, Gloria's jaw dropped. She knew exactly what had happened. Todd had *understood* her. As unbelievable as it seemed, she had actually communicated a clear and important message to her son! She had broken through the teen barrier!

She looked at Joel. He was smiling. He started to say, "So I guess he's more level headed than--," when, suddenly, a flicker in the CF/RQ window caught Gloria's eye. She held up a hand, halting Joel in mid-sentence, and stared at the window. Sure enough, it did it again.

Just as with the last message, the RQ reading flickered. The 48% flashed, then changed to 42%, 26% then 7%, and then back to 48%.

As it was happening this time, Gloria also glanced at the RECEIVER plate and noticed something else. The picture of her was changing subtly every time the RQ reading flickered. Her face was changing. Instead of fear and frustration, in those instances when the RQ reading got lower, her face appeared to have a crafty and sly expression on it. As she looked still closer, she realized that the stranger was changing too. He was talking - saying something to her. *He* suddenly seemed to be the one trying to communicate, and she looked utterly wicked!

A sinking feeling crept into Gloria's stomach. She thought she might have an idea of what was happening, but hoped she was wrong. She turned quickly to Joel. "What's going on?" she asked.

Joel was leaning back, a pained, spaced-out look on his face. In a strange, high-pitched voice, he said, "It's just the opposite!"

"What?" Gloria said, suddenly becoming very frightened.

"The boy is *talking opposite*!" Joel continued, "Four's important now!"

Gloria looked quickly back and forth -- her face on the plate looking frightened, frustrated ... Joel, with a strained, high-pitched voice ... her face on the plate looking wicked, mean ... the stranger, his lips moving, his face changing from sinister to meek.

Joel continued, "*Please*! It's just the opposite! Four is the magic number!"

Gloria was nearing hysteria. "Joel! Joel, what do you mean?! Talk sense to me! *Please!*"

"He's talking *Three reversed!*"

"Joel! Joel!"

"Listen! *Two and two's the key! The opposite of three!*"

Gloria panicked and reached for Joel. Her hands went through his face and she tumbled into a pool of warm, black sludge. She tried to gain her footing and climb out, but couldn't. The sludge was pulling, sucking at her body, dragging her under. She struggled, grasped, and came up with handfulls of paper and plastic. Floating on the surface of the muck were hundreds of calculators, electric guitars and sports pages! She screamed, sank under, and suddenly came wide awake, sitting on her bed. She was drenched in sweat.

Staring into the darkness of her bedroom, she had no precise recollection of what had scared her so badly. She only knew that she felt as if she had been very close to discovering something important and suddenly it had transformed into a horrible nightmare.

CHAPTER 11

THE DAYS BEFORE DISCOVERY

ALTHOUGH SHE NEVER fully remembered it, Gloria had the same dream for the next six nights.

Each time, she would be with Joel and Todd. Joel would explain about speaking in ways that were hard for the listener to distort.

She would send the same message to Todd and it would seem to get through. Then the CF/RQ window would flicker. The numbers would change. The picture would change. Joel would go crazy ... sludge ... sweat ... horror ... her dark bedroom.

On the morning after the fourth night, Gloria became very depressed. She had no idea what kept waking her, or why. The days were becoming unsettled, too. Everything she did seemed to have an awkwardness or incompleteness to it, as if some vital part of her life was being torn away. Anxious thoughts about Bill and uncomfortable memories of her parents kept creeping into her mind as well. She was beginning to think something was very wrong with her.

It was on the seventh day that the crisis finally provided the answer.

CHAPTER 12

FINALLY UNDERSTANDING

It was Saturday. Bill had been out of town for two days. He was taking an early flight home from Dallas that morning. Gloria had just finished balancing the checkbook and was on her way to the kitchen for a cup of coffee.

The first indication that something was very wrong occurred as she passed Todd's room and heard music playing. She looked at her watch. It was only 8:20 a.m. There was no way he should be up so early, Gloria thought.

At first she decided to let it pass, but as she moved by his bedroom door, she began to get a sensation of déjà vu.

The sensation was nothing out of the ordinary, she thought, at least not recently. It was the same thing she had been experiencing for weeks. Most of the time, it had been accompanied by a positive kind of feeling. Lately, though, it had been just the opposite. *'Opposite,'* she thought. What was it about that word? She stopped in her tracks. In addition to the music, she thought she could also hear movement. She knocked.

No answer.

She knocked again and called out, "Todd, honey?"

Still no answer. Fear gripped her. She opened the door and stepped in. The feeling of déjà vu immediately intensified.

Todd was seated cross-legged beside his stereo. He was turned away from Gloria, staring out the window. Most of his dresser drawers were pulled open and two stacks of his clothes were lying in the middle of the floor. His backpack was also out on the floor laying wide open. Beside it were his two beloved harmonicas lying on a picture of Trudy, his girlfriend.

Gloria's mind raced. She immediately began putting two and two together and they added up to a number she didn't like.

Two and two? she suddenly thought. Those numbers. There was something about--!

She could feel herself starting to hyperventilate. Just as she was about to ask what was going on (the only logical question, although she already knew the answer), Todd turned from the window and, in a very calm but sad voice, said, "I'm leaving home."

Suddenly, the past few days of discomfort and the sensations of déjà vu began to make some odd kind of sense to Gloria. She wasn't sure how, but she'd had a premonition this was coming. She hadn't been sleeping because she had been worried about Todd or had dreamed about him, or something. She couldn't put her finger on it, but she was absolutely sure she was right.

And she was sure of something else. Somehow, she knew exactly what to do. She had the power to change what was happening. And gaining that power had been a part of these strange few weeks.

As people often do in stressful situations, she acted on what appeared to be instinct. Instinct, however, was not really the case. In reality, Gloria began to act on a series of very important lessons she had recently learned.

The first thing she needed became clear at once. She had to get Todd's complete attention. What would come after that she wasn't sure, but she did know that they had to connect and they had to do it clearly. She had to be able to express what she really felt to her son and she had to do it right now, before it was too late. She sat down on the bed and took a deep breath.

"Todd," she said. His eyes were empty and dark. They found hers and held. "You need to stop thinking about everything else and listen to what I have to say. It's more important than you realize. Will you please do that for me?"

His eyes held on hers for a long moment. She could tell that he understood. She had gotten through as she somehow knew she would. It was going to be okay. The déjà vu told her that he was just about to nod his head and agree with her.

Then, just as Gloria was about to continue, something in Todd's face changed. The understanding left his eyes as if suddenly swept away in a flash of anger and suspicion. "No, Mom," he said, "that's not what's important now."

Gloria was stunned. It *was* what was needed. She was sure of it! Something told her she had to talk to him and talk clearly. The déjà vu! It had already happened this way! She had to express exactly what was on her mind in precise terms. Todd was wrong. She had to clarify her feelings to save him. To keep him home! Something else was wrong - terribly wrong. The fear suddenly began to take over.

"What we need, Mom," Todd said, "is exactly the opposite."

Opposite! That word again. What was it about that word. She had heard it before, just recently. But where? When? She had ... he ... he was .... "Wha ... what?" she muttered, barely able to talk.

"What *you* need to do first," he said, "is *listen*."

"Listen." "Four is the key." "The boy is talking Opposite." A cyclone of thoughts, emotions, and questions raced through Gloria's mind. What was Number Four? Why did everything sound so familiar? Where had she heard all this? Why wasn't she supposed to talk? She *was* supposed to talk. She was supposed to talk with perfect clarity. She was supposed to break through the teen barrier. She was....

And then it hit her.

He was right. She was supposed to talk and she would, but not now. Now, she was supposed to do the *opposite.* She was supposed to *listen.* It was a lesson of some kind. The fourth lesson. Yes. She was not supposed to talk with clarity, but *listen* with clarity – allow her son to penetrate *her* barrier. Of course!

Then, in a sudden flood of deja vu, she imagined something else. It was a message unfolding in her mind:

LISTEN WITH CLARITY
✓ EMPATHIZE
✓ VISUALIZE

In the next few seconds, this uncanny realization continued to unfold. Listening with clarity, she realized, meant listening to her son, without distorting what he was about to say by hearing it through her own opinions, values, or past experiences. She had to put her personal opinions and values aside. She had to *empathize* with him - put herself in his position as he spoke, and *visualize* - try very hard to imagine exactly what he was 'seeing' as he spoke.

Like so many other things happening recently, she wasn't sure exactly what was going on or why, but she was positive this was exactly what was needed.

How simple, she thought. How perfect. It was like discovering the final piece of some amazing communication puzzle. Not expressing or concentrating on *her* point of view, but reversing roles - the opposite. Listening to what the other person wanted to express. *Really* listening!

Letting their message play out with perfect clarity in her mind. *Understanding!*

She realized how seldom she had done that - actually sat, listened, and truly understood. Not only with Todd, but with everyone she was associated with. And what little listening she had done had been distorted. The words had been changed, made into something they weren't by the opinions and preferences she'd formed over the years. The words had become what *she* wanted to hear, not what people had been trying to say to her. Just as she'd formed a distorted image of Martin Shelby, she'd done the same with her son. Todd wasn't the terrible person she'd come to believe. He was just a boy. A young man growing up, inching his way through the confusing and often painful process of turning into a man. When the path had been difficult or frightening, he'd called out for help, and Gloria realized now how rarely she had stepped in to offer the security and stability he'd needed so desperately. She'd been so intent on being heard, so determined to be listened to and respected that she had talked constantly. And suddenly, this realization brought back that same familiar image from her childhood. The breakfast table. Her father and mother. Her *mother!* The small talk. The words that had gone on and on and meant so little. The misdirected attempts to be heard. *Listened* to. Just like. . .*Gloria!*

And so, with a profound and crystal clear understanding of *herself*, for the first time in years, Gloria listened, *really* listened to her son. And she was able to imagine what Todd was saying with a clarity that truly amazed her.

When he said he had felt trapped and frustrated because she would never consider his point of view, she didn't take offense or go immediately to her opinions in self-defense. Instead, she was able to "see" his frustration in her own mind. She was able to "feel" the horrible knot in *her* stomach that he had felt in his when he had tried on so many occasions to "reach" her. She was able to empathize and visualize, and she was overwhelmed by the intense feeling of power and well-being it brought to her.

Todd knew it was happening, too. When he talked about his loneliness, and the fears and confusion a teenage boy feels as he slowly turns into a man, he knew that this time she understood. He could feel the images leaving his mouth with exactly the right phrasing and forming perfectly painted pictures in his mother's mind.

And later, when the time was right, Gloria talked also. She talked with the same perfect clarity to her son, and he listened. He empathized, visualized, and understood. How hurt and afraid his mother had felt when she couldn't reach him. How separated she had felt when he had isolated himself in music and seeming indifference. How betrayed she had felt when he had lashed out at her.

When the conversation was nearly over, the final bit of communication healing fell into place.

Both she and Todd heard a noise and looked up. Bill was standing in the doorway, suitcase still in hand.

How long he had been there neither one knew. But he was smiling. He must have heard a great deal of what had been said because the look in his eyes told Gloria and Todd that, he too, realized something wonderful was happening.

He "saw".

He understood.

"Any chance a dad and husband who's been gone from home a little too long can get in on what's happening here?" he asked.

CHAPTER 13

CLARITY IN A CAPSULE

ONE NIGHT NEARLY a week later, Gloria kissed Bill and rolled over in bed. She was about to turn off the light when she suddenly had a thought. She got up.

She went to her briefcase, opened it, and got out her daily planner. She flipped to the notes section at the back and opened it to the page containing her communication notes.

Those notes had now become a short but complete summary of the entire process she had discovered. She looked it over briefly, took out a pen and wrote in the final few words - a title. When she was done, the entire summary read:

THE CLARITY FACTOR:

The Clarity Factor is a simple, four-step method used to clarify verbal communication. The Clarity Factor assumes that clear speech has a *visual* quality which can be brought more (or less) into focus, depending on how the communication is stated.

The Clarity Factor defines a verbal communication as a *message*. It defines the speaker of that message as the *sender*, and it defines the person listening to the message as the *receiver*.

The Clarity Factor can be stated as follows:

THE CLARITY FACTOR
A measure of how clearly a person
speaks and listens based on
four key Focal Points

THE CLARITY FOCAL POINTS:

1. Focus Your Message

In order to speak with clarity, the person talking must first clarify their thoughts at the source - in their own mind. This is accomplished through:

Analysis - Thinking over and deciding exactly what needs to be said. This sharpens focus.

Objectivity - Removing personal emotions. This limits distortion and increases accuracy.

2. Magnify The Listener's Attention

Once the person speaking has clarified their words at the source, the next step is to motivate the listener into giving top priority to the speaker. This is accomplished by assuring that the message communicates one or all of the following:

Interest -	Subject matter of interest to the receiver.
Importance -	Subject matter of importance to the receiver.
A request for the receiver's undivided attention-	Asking the receiver to stop what he or she is doing and please listen carefully.

3. PENETRATE PERSONAL BARRIERS

Once the person speaking has the listener's attention, the message can be sent. The object at this point is to assure that it gets through as close as possible to the way the *speaker* has visualized it. The listener's own personal opinions, values, and past experiences will act as personal barriers or "distortion factors" to this process. The speaker, however, can greatly disable these distortion factors, thus assuring that the message gets through with maximum clarity. This is accomplished with the use of:

Visual Language -	Using visual and precise word choices and phrases.
Analogies -	Stating the message according to a reference common to both the speaker and the listener.

Request for feedback - Asking the listener if the message is clear.

Revision as needed - Revising the message based on feedback from the receiver.

4. LISTEN WITH CLARITY

Perhaps the most rewarding part of the Clarity Factor comes when the speaker gains the ability to reverse roles and become a clarity *receiver* or listener -- in other words, truly understanding the speaker's message by letting down their own personal barriers and receiving it on *the speaker's terms.* This process of understanding is accomplished when the listener is able to:

Empathize - Place himself or herself in the speaker's position.

Visualize - Imagine what the speaker is trying to communicate.

Gloria closed her daily planner and smiled. Yes, she decided, she had truly discovered a method of communicating that was deceptively simple but amazingly effective. And having gained that knowledge, she realized she'd crossed an important bridge as a manager, a wife and a mother. She'd finally come to understand her world and the people who occupied it. It was no longer necessary to be defensive and closed, to control the actions and personalities of those surrounding her in order to validate her own needs. She could open up now and let go of her insecurities and fear of failure. And she knew that knowledge would be equally valuable to her both on the job and in her home.

She'd found true confidence in herself through an understanding of others.

She went back to bed, snuggled up comfortably, and turned out the light. A fond image of her parents drifted peacefully into her mind. Two wonderful people who had been such loving parents and lifelong soul mates. Had they only known what she had finally discovered.

With this thought in mind, she fell asleep and began to dream....

CHAPTER 14

A FINAL MEETING

SHE FOUND HIM seated on a park bench.

She had no idea what park it was or where it was, but it was beautiful. Huge elms and eucalyptus were scattered everywhere. As far as the eye could see, the land was a rolling green expanse of sun-washed hills.

People picnicked, kids played with kites and Frisbees, and dogs jumped and ran. As she and Joel began to talk, a steady stream of people of all ages and races moved past them along a narrow cobbled walkway.

The Clarity Monitoring System was on the bench beside Joel. Gloria sat down. "Why didn't you *tell* me number four was the opposite of number three - to listen with clarity?" she asked.

Joel smiled and said, "*Would* you have listened?"

Gloria smiled. A gentle breeze picked up. "So what now?"

"Now," Joel said, "you take the Clarity Factor out of dreamsville and you start sharing it with other people who need it. You spread some of that hard-earned understanding of yours around."

"And how about you?"

"Same thing. I find some other unsuspecting person whose mind I can crawl into after dark."

Gloria hesitated. "We'll never see each other again?" she asked.

Joel looked into her eyes. He said nothing.

"Then before we part ways," Gloria said, "please stop everything you're doing. Look at me and listen. I have something very important to tell you."

Joel smiled.

Gloria turned to the Clarity Monitoring System and began to type. As she did, two images moved out of the stream of passing people - one image was Gloria and the other was Joel. They walked to a spot under the elm tree right beside the real Gloria and Joel and stopped. They stood quietly, looking into each other's eyes. When Gloria finished typing, she pushed the TRANSMIT button.

The image of her smiled and said to the image of Joel, "Joel, before you go away, please talk to me. Tell me all about who you are, and where you're from. I want to hear what you think and feel about me and you and the world and people and dreams. I want very much, Joel, to just *listen* to you. I want to understand you and your world, because you've shown me that understanding my world and the people in it is the most rewarding experience a human being can achieve."

The Image Plates came to life. Gloria didn't look. She knew what the pictures in both plates would be.

Instead, she looked at Joel. He, too, knew what the images in the plates would be. He simply reached over, pushed a button, and turned off the system.

As the Clarity Monitoring System slowly wound down with a final deepening whine, Joel turned to Gloria and smiled. He hesitated for a moment, then said, "Before I start, I want you to think back. Later in your life. Around the time you returned home for a short visit after college. Do you recall seeing that Sports section at the breakfast table any more?"

Gloria searched her memory. The image came crystal clear. Most things were the same. Sunlight. Warmth. The kitchen table. Her parents were there and all three of them were older.

And. . .there was no Sports section! She and her parents smiled and talked. Breakfast was a happy, comfortable time. . .a time of shared ideas and smiles and personal recognition. . .a time of truth and understanding. *Understanding*. . .a time of. . . "*Clarity*!" she suddenly said out loud.

"Turns out your mother was quite a dreamer," Joel said, smiling gently.

Tears came to Gloria's eyes.

"And still is, by the way. . ."

"Thank you," Gloria said.

"You're welcome. . .Now, as for me. The truth is, it all began in the year ... well, let's just say a long, long ... *long* time ago...."

ABOUT THE AUTHOR

RAY DIZAZZO IS an author, communication consultant, screenwriter, poet and seminar speaker. *The Clarity Factor* is Mr. DiZazzo's seventh book. He has appeared on radio and television and taught the Clarity Factor principles to major companies in the U.S. and abroad. Mr. DiZazzo and his wife of 45 years live in southern California. He continues to write, speak and as he puts it, *"...do everything in my power to help people discover the amazing, simple and often untapped power of true clarity."*

Made in the USA
Monee, IL
12 August 2022

10727128R00069